THE FIRST MEN WHO WENT TO THE MOON

BY **RHONDA GOWLER GREENE** ILLUSTRATED BY **SCOTT BRUNDAGE**

PUBLISHED BY SLEEPING BEAR PRESS

These are the first men who went to the Moon.

Lunar Module Pilot
Edwin "Buzz" Aldrin

Command Module Pilot
Michael Collins

Commander
Neil Armstrong

NO SMOKING

APOLLO II

This is the spacecraft, Apollo 11,
that lifted off and soared through the heavens
and carried the first men who went to the Moon.

On July 16, 1969, at 9:32 a.m. EDT, Apollo 11
lifted off from Cape Kennedy, Florida. The spacecraft
sat atop the giant Saturn V launch vehicle.

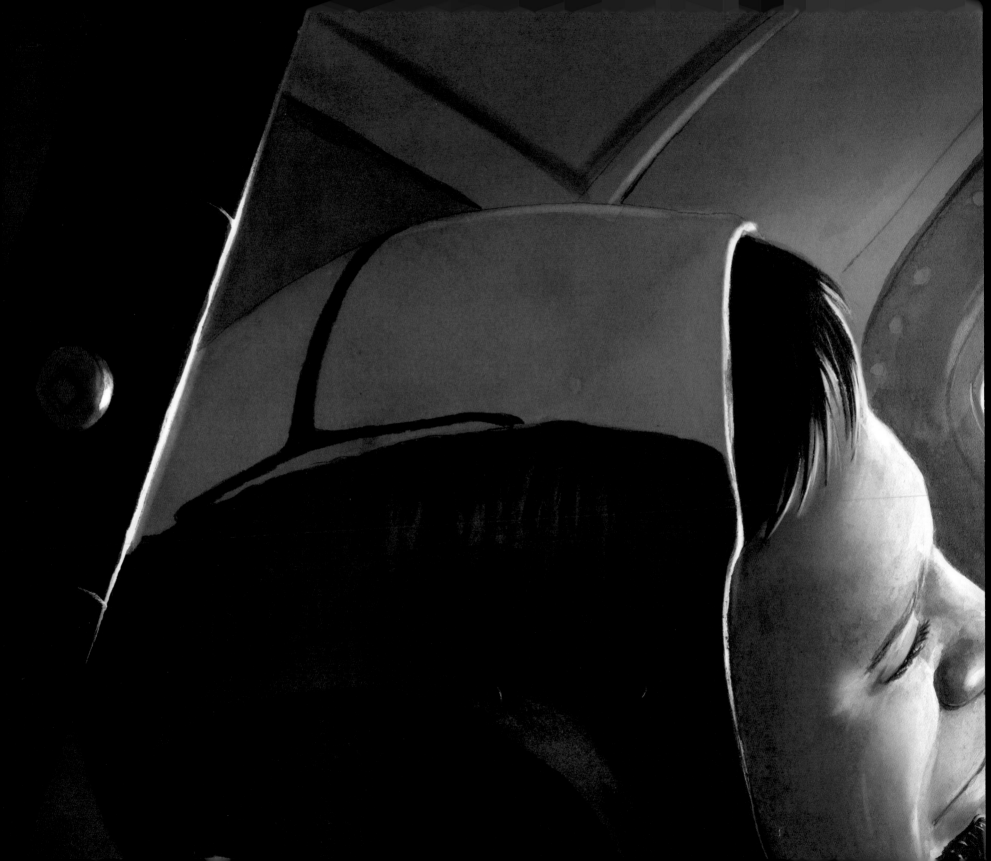

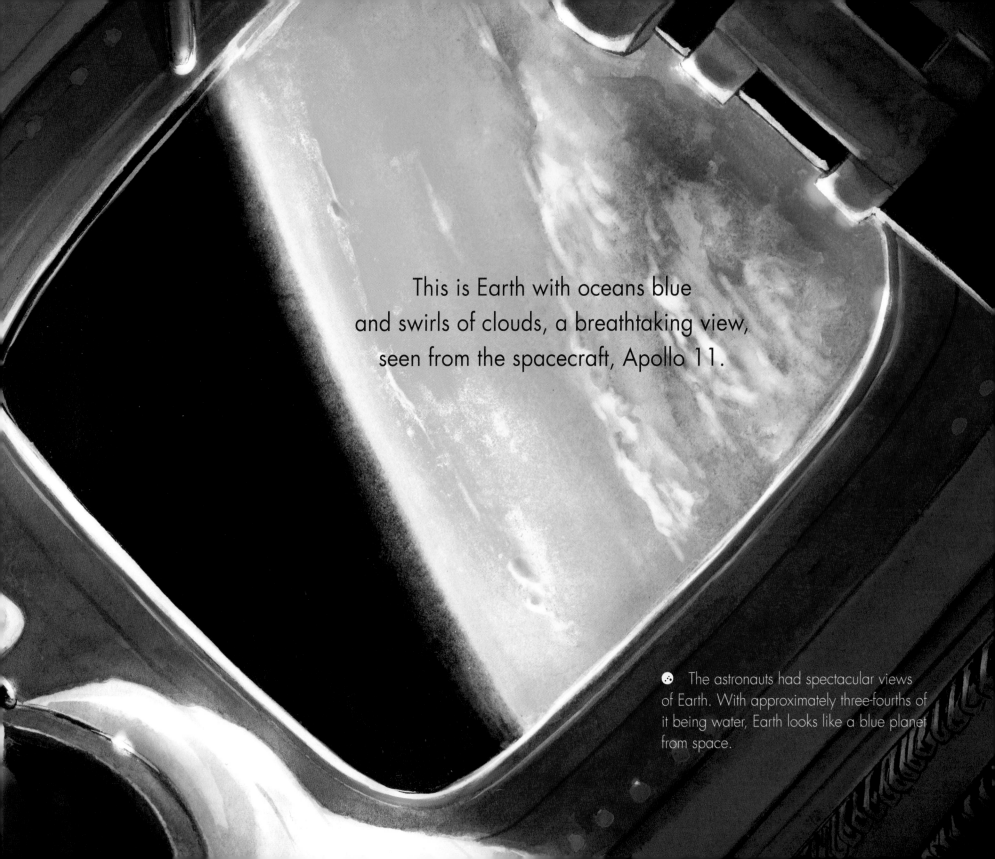

This is Earth with oceans blue
and swirls of clouds, a breathtaking view,
seen from the spacecraft, Apollo 11.

The astronauts had spectacular views
of Earth. With approximately three-fourths of
it being water, Earth looks like a blue planet
from space.

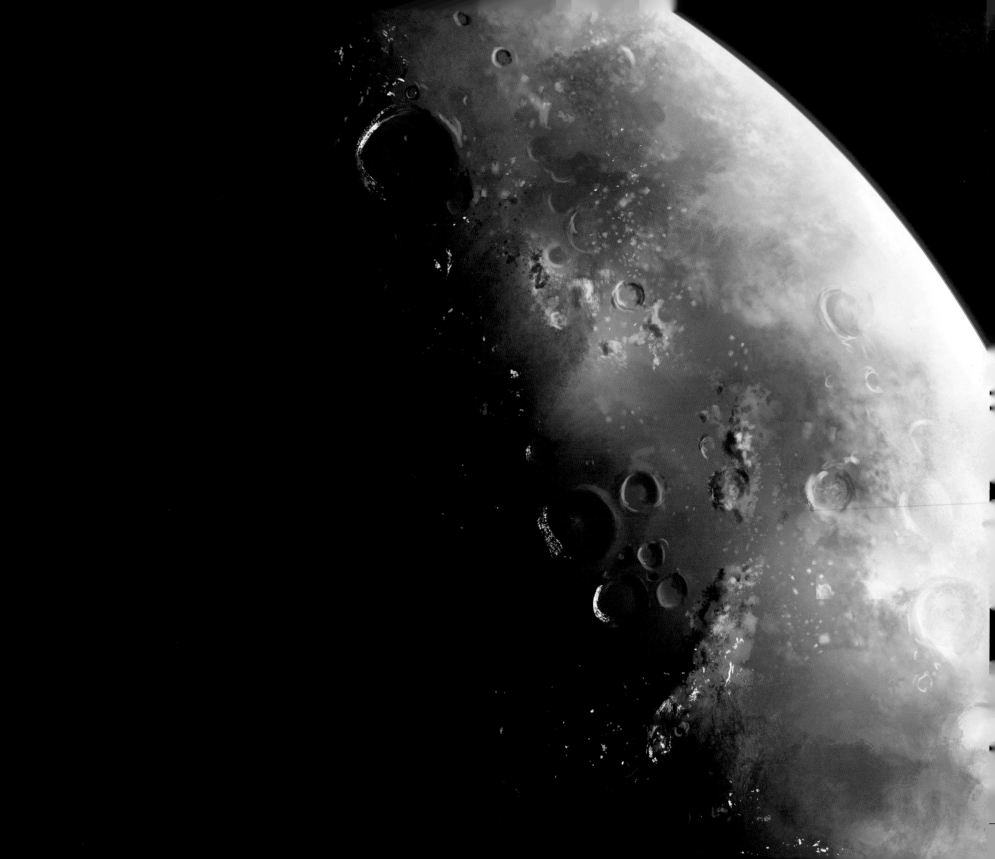

This is the Moon, a mysterious place,
a desolate land in the darkness of space,
far from Earth with oceans blue.

Four days after liftoff, Apollo 11 reached the Moon, approximately 239,000 miles away. Unlike Earth, the Moon has only trace amounts of air and water, making it a barren and uninhabitable place.

This is the *Eagle* that set men down
to walk the dust of lunar ground
and explore the Moon, a mysterious place.

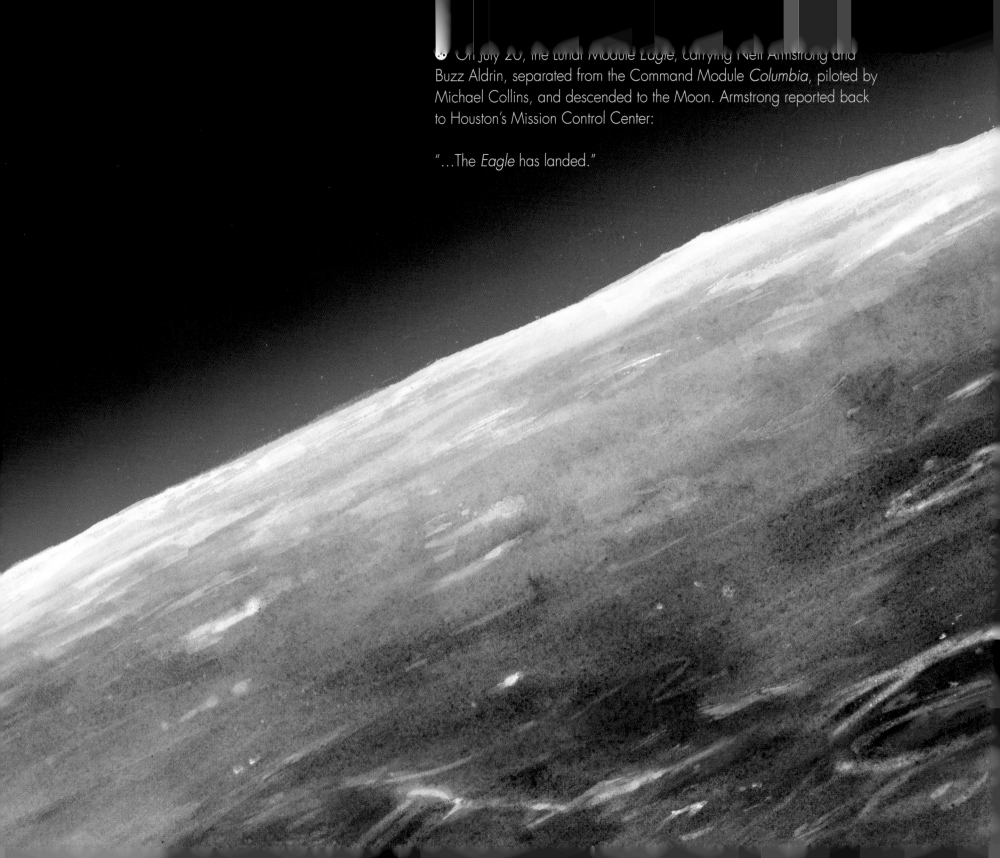

On July 20, the Lunar Module *Eagle*, carrying Neil Armstrong and Buzz Aldrin, separated from the Command Module *Columbia*, piloted by Michael Collins, and descended to the Moon. Armstrong reported back to Houston's Mission Control Center:

"...The *Eagle* has landed."

This is the Sea of Tranquility
where the astronauts made history
when they stepped from the *Eagle* that set men down.

This is their mark, a "leap for mankind."
And this is the flag they left behind
there in the Sea of Tranquility.

⊙ Neil Armstrong was the first human to set foot on the Moon. These were his words heard round
the world: "That's one small step for man, one giant leap for mankind."

Buzz Aldrin soon followed. While on the Moon, Armstrong and Aldrin set up scientific equipment,
took photographs, gathered rock and soil samples, and planted an American flag. After a rest period
in *Eagle*, they lifted off in the ascent stage and docked with *Columbia*.

They left a plaque on the Moon with these words—

HERE MEN FROM THE PLANET EARTH
FIRST SET FOOT UPON THE MOON
JULY 1969, A.D.
WE CAME IN PEACE FOR ALL MANKIND

This is the splashdown that brought them home,
safe and sound from a vast unknown,
where they made their mark, a "leap for mankind."

On July 24, at 12:51 p.m. EDT, *Columbia* splashed down in the Pacific Ocean. Armstrong, Aldrin, and Collins were picked up by helicopter and flown to the aircraft carrier USS *Hornet*, which transported them to the naval station at Pearl Harbor in Hawaii.

The first Moon walk mission was a success.

This is the welcome that everyone gave
to those three men, so daring and brave,

after the splashdown that brought them home,
safe and sound from a vast unknown,

August 13, 1969
New York City (and Chicago)

where they made their mark, a "leap for mankind."
And this is the flag they left behind

there in the Sea of Tranquility
where the astronauts made history

when they stepped from the *Eagle* that set men down
to walk the dust of lunar ground

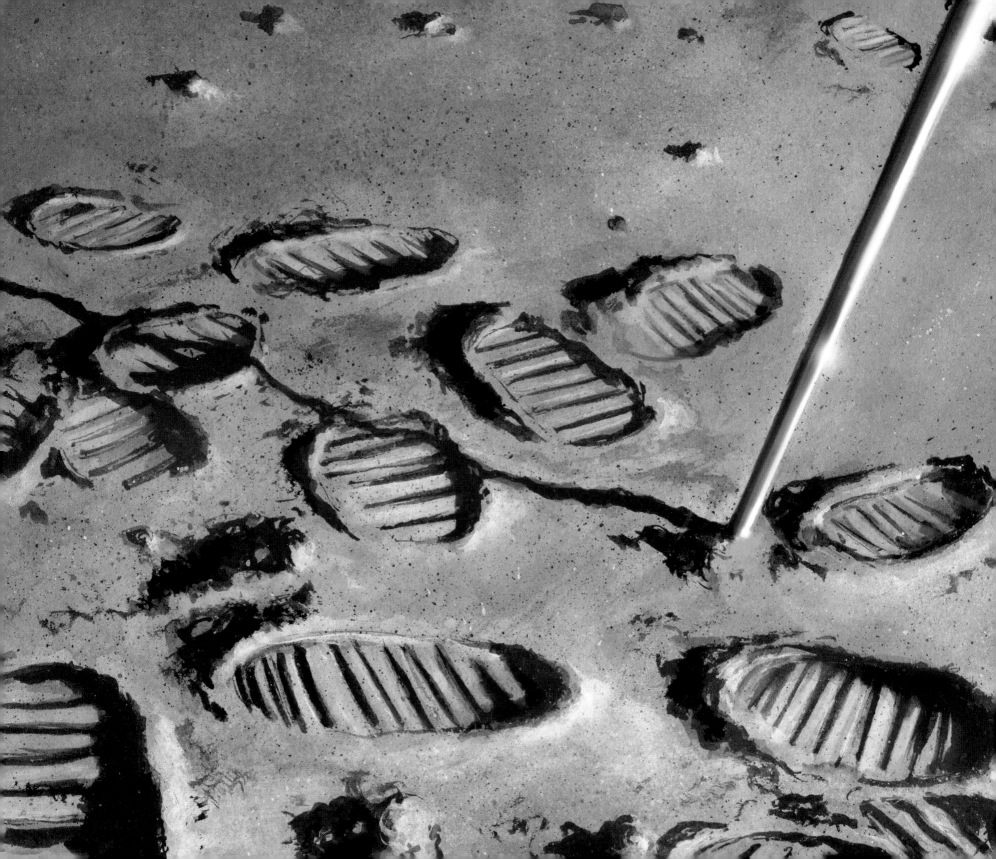

and explore the Moon, a mysterious place,
a desolate land in the darkness of space,

far from Earth with oceans blue
and swirls of clouds, a breathtaking view,

and carried the first men who went to the Moon.

Where are *Eagle* and *Columbia* now?

☾ The descent stage (lower section) of the Lunar Module *Eagle* was left on the Moon. The ascent stage (upper section) lifted off the Moon on July 21, 1969, transporting Armstrong and Aldrin back to *Columbia*. Programmed to crash to the Moon, the ascent stage then jettisoned from *Columbia* into temporary lunar orbit. Its exact impact site is unknown.

☾ Except for infrequent touring exhibits in select US cities, the Command Module *Columbia* calls the Smithsonian's National Air and Space Museum in Washington, DC, its home.

More About the Mission and the Moon

☾ In 1961, in a speech to Congress, President John F. Kennedy challenged the United States to land a man on the Moon and return him safely to Earth by the end of the decade. The goal was met with Apollo 11. Sadly, President Kennedy did not live to see it happen.

☾ The powerful three-stage Saturn V launch vehicle was approximately 36 stories high and, when fully fueled, weighed 6.2 million pounds.

☾ The last minutes of *Eagle*'s descent to the Moon were tense—alarms sounded, fuel was running low, a crater and large boulders loomed. Armstrong manually took over the controls, flew beyond the crater, and quickly located a smooth surface for landing.

☾ When Neil Armstrong stepped on the Moon, the words the world was supposed to have heard were: "That's one small step for *a* man, one giant leap for mankind." It remains uncertain whether the *a* was accidentally omitted or lost in transmission.

☾ President Richard M. Nixon spoke to the astronauts from the Oval Office by radiotelephone while they were on the Moon.

☾ The astronauts' space suits were crucial for survival. They not only provided oxygen, but served as protection from the Moon's extreme temperatures, which range from about 250 degrees Fahrenheit in direct sunlight to about minus 380 degrees Fahrenheit in regions of permanent darkness.

☾ Aldrin stepped on the Moon 19 minutes after Armstrong. The astronauts walked on the Moon for about 2.5 hours. Once back inside *Eagle*, they had a rest period of 7 hours before ascending to dock with *Columbia*.

For my brother, Steve. Thanks for asking me to watch the first Moon landing and walk on live TV with you.
—Rhonda

To my mom, the strongest person I know
—Scott

Sleeping Bear Press™

2395 South Huron Parkway, Suite 200
Ann Arbor, MI 48104
www.sleepingbearpress.com
© Sleeping Bear Press
Printed and bound in the United States
10 9 8 7 6 5 4 3 2 1
Library of Congress Cataloging-in-Publication Data
Names: Greene, Rhonda Gowler, author. | Brundage, Scott, illustrator.
Title: The first men who went to the moon
written by Rhonda Gowler Greene ; illustrated by Scott Brundage.
Description: Ann Arbor, MI : Sleeping Bear Press, [2019] | Audience: Ages 6-10.
Identifiers: LCCN 2018037163 | ISBN 9781585364121 (hardcover)
Subjects: LCSH: Project Apollo (U.S.)–Juvenile literature. | Armstrong,
Neil, 1930-2012–Juvenile literature. | Aldrin, Buzz–Juvenile literature.
Collins, Michael, 1930—Juvenile literature. | Apollo 11
(Spacecraft)–Juvenile literature. | Space flight to the moon–Juvenile
literature. | Moon–Exploration–Juvenile literature.
Classification: LCC TL789.8.U6 G35845 2019 | DDC 629.45/4/0973–dc23
LC record available at https://lccn.loc.gov/2018037163